A N(

Prayer Book

*All booklets are published thanks to the
generous support of the members of the
Catholic Truth Society*

CATHOLIC TRUTH SOCIETY
PUBLISHERS TO THE HOLY SEE

Contents

Preface

Thanks to the Catholic Truth Society this selection of prayers and meditations by John Henry Newman is, in time for his beatification, being made available in this new edition. These are the prayers that helped make Newman a saint. They certainly make his sanctity clear to us.

Newman chose for his cardinal's motto a phrase from the writings of St Francis de Sales, a saint who, like Newman himself, founded an Oratory, a place of prayer. That motto, *Heart speaks to Heart*, sums up the spirit of Newman's life of prayer. Every word here comes from John Henry Newman's heart. The language is beautiful but also simple and direct. The thought is profound but nothing is obscure. He is praying for consolation, to be able to bear suffering, for his friends, for a happy death. These might be our own prayers.

We are consoled to find that a saint has the same concerns that we have. But we are also led more deeply into prayer because saints see more clearly what really matters. They penetrate to the heart of things and they know what we need to ask for.

These prayers give us a unique entry into the prayer life of a saint, the words of his heart as he spoke to the Heart of God. They draw us, so to speak, into the conversation, and invite us to make the prayers our own. So while John Henry Newman's heart speaks to God, his heart also speaks to ours.

In his life, John Henry Newman was a friend, teacher and priest to many people. And it is still so for us today. We recognise him as a friend, because his concerns are ours as well. We know him to be a teacher because he leads us always to a deeper knowledge of the truth. And we find him still to be a priest, through his prayer for us. In short, heart speaks to heart.

I hope that many will find a friend, a teacher and a priest in these words of the soon to be Blessed, John Henry Newman.

Fr Richard Duffield
Provost of the Birmingham Oratory

John Henry Newman, 1801-1890

John Henry Newman was born on 21st February 1801 in London. At school he underwent a conversion and after taking his degree was elected Fellow of Oriel College, Oxford. He became Vicar of the University Church, and after 1833 leader of the Oxford Movement, dedicated to the sacramental and spiritual renewal of the Church of England. His religious influence, nourished by his studies of the first Christian centuries, was extensive but controversial.

Increasingly convinced that the Protestant Reformation had been mistaken, and that the Church of England could not be uprooted from its Reformation origins, Newman underwent a long interior struggle, culminating in his retirement to Littlemore, outside Oxford, where he lived in dedication to discerning the will of God. At last he came to see that the Roman Catholic Church was the 'One Fold of Christ.' Newman was received into the Catholic Church by Blessed Dominic Barberi on 9th October 1845.

Ordained a priest in Rome, Newman returned to England with a Papal commission to found houses of the Oratorian Congregation in England, in Birmingham and then in London. He became the first Rector of the Catholic University in Ireland and founded the Oratory School in Birmingham. Working tirelessly especially for the poor parishioners of the Birmingham Oratory, Newman also carried on an enormous correspondence, helping countless people from all over the world with their religious difficulties.

His theological and philosophical writings retain a profound influence upon our own times, especially his theory of the development of doctrine, his explorations of the relation between Faith and reason, and his challenging argument that the light of conscience is fulfilled and perfected in obedience to the teaching of the Catholic Church.

When in 1879 Pope Leo XIII made him a cardinal, Newman said that his great aim had been opposition to religious liberalism, by which he meant the view that Christianity is a matter of sentiment or opinion rather than truth. Praised for his unstinting care of souls, humility and prayerful contact with the invisible world, he died in Birmingham on 11 August 1890.

Morning Prayers

LORD, I thank you that you have brought me to the beginning of this day, defend me in the same by your mighty power, and grant as I now rise after sleep, fresh and rejoicing, so my body after the sleep of death may rise spiritualized and blessed to dwell with you forever.

Keep me from the perils and dangers of this day; let me fall into no sin, neither run into any kind of danger, but let all my doings be ordered by your governance, to do always what is righteous in your sight, through Jesus Christ our Saviour.

ALMIGHTY GOD and Father of our Lord Jesus Christ, who day by day renews your mercies to sinful man, accept, I pray you, this morning sacrifice of praise and thanksgiving, and give me grace to offer it reverently, and in humble faith, and with a willing mind.

I praise you for my birth from kind and anxious parents; for your gifts of health and reason; for your continued care of me, for my baptism into your Holy Church, and every measure of your grace granted to me; for your gracious forgiveness of all my sins. Also I praise and magnify your name for every affliction and anxiety you have laid, or now lay upon me, and I acknowledge thankfully that hitherto all has worked for good.

Evening Prayers

LORD, I thank you that you have safely brought me to the end of this day. Protect me from the perils and dangers of the night. Let me rest in peace. Let me lay myself down gratefully as if in death, knowing my spirit may this night be required of me; give me grace that whenever that time comes I may be prepared for it and that when my soul parts from this body, it may hear the grateful words "Well done, thou good and faithful servant, enter into the joy of your Lord."

O GOD, give me grace at this time duly to confess my sins before you, and truly to repent of them. Blot out of your book, gracious Lord, all my manifold acts of sin committed against you. Forgive me all my wanderings in prayer, my sins of omission, my deliberate sins against conscience.

Give me eyes to see what is right, and a heart to follow it, and strength to perform it; and grant that I may in all things press forward in the work of sanctification and ever do your will, and at length through your mercy attain to the glories of your everlasting kingdon through Jesus Christ our Lord.

Prayers for Each Day of the Month

First Day

A Prayer to the Eternal God

TO POSSESS you, Lover of Souls, is happiness, and the only happiness of the immortal soul. To enjoy the sight of you is the only happiness of eternity. What can give me happiness but you? To see you, to contemplate you, this alone is inexhaustible. You indeed are unchangeable, yet in you there are always more glorious depths and more varied attributes to search into; we shall ever be beginning as if we had never gazed upon you. How far am I from acting according to what I know so well! Rouse me from sloth and coldness, and make me desire you with my whole heart.

Second Day

A Prayer of Adoration

MY GOD, I adore you, as holy in all your works as well as in your own nature. No creature can approach your incommunicable sanctity, but you approach, and touch, and possess, all creatures; and nothing lives but in you, and nothing have you created but what is good.

I adore you as having created man upright, and having bountifully given him an integrity of nature, and having filled him with your free grace, so that he was like an Angel upon earth; and I adore you, for having given him your grace over again in still more measure, and with far more lasting fruits, through your Eternal Son incarnate. In all your works you are holy, and I adore you in them all.

Third Day

A Prayer of Desire

MY GOD, you are my life; if I leave you, I cannot but thirst. Lost spirits thirst, in hell, because they have not God. I wish to be clad in that new nature, which so longs for you from loving you, as to overcome in me the fear of coming to you. I come to you, Lord, not only because I am unhappy without you, not only because I feel I need you, but because your grace draws me on to seek you. I come in great fear, but in greater love. As years pass away, and the heart shuts up, and all things are a burden, let me never lose this youthful, eager love of you. The more I refuse to open my heart to you, so much the fuller and stronger be your supernatural visitings, and the more urgent and efficacious your presence within me.

Fourth Day

A Prayer of Trust in God

GOD HAS created me to do him some definite service; he has committed some work to me which he has not committed to another. I have my mission - I may never know it in this life, but I shall be told it in the next. I am a link in a chain, a bond of connection between persons. He has not created me for naught. I shall do good, I shall do his work; I shall be a preacher of truth in my own place, while not intending it, if I do but keep his commandments and serve him in my calling.

Therefore, my God, I will put myself without reserve into your hands. What have I in heaven, and apart from you what do I want upon earth? My flesh and my heart fail, but God is the God of my heart, and my portion for ever.

Fifth Day

A Prayer for the Church on Earth

BE WITH your missionaries in pagan lands, put right words into their mouths, prosper their labours, and sustain them under their sufferings with your consolations, and carry them on to their reward in heaven. Give the grace of wisdom to those in high station, that they may neither yield to fear, nor be seduced by flattery. Give your blessing to all preachers and teachers, that they may speak your words and persuade their hearers to love you. Be with all faithful servants of yours, whether in low station or in high. Teach us, one and all, to live in your presence and to see you, our Great Leader and your Cross.

Sixth Day

A Prayer for an Increase of Love

MY LORD, I believe, and know, and feel, that you are the Supreme Good. I believe that beautiful as is your creation, it is of no account compared with you. And therefore, since I perceive you to be so beautiful, I love you, and desire to love you more and more. My God, you know how little I love you. I should not love you at all, except for your grace. Keep my whole being fixed on you. Let me never lose sight of you; and let my love for you grow more and more every day.

Seventh Day

A Prayer of Praise to the Holy Spirit,
the Life of All Things

I ADORE you, my Lord and my God, the Eternal Paraclete, co-equal with the Father and the Son. Through you, the earth was brought into its present state, and was matured to be a habitation for man. Through you, Almighty Lord, the angels and saints sing to you praises in heaven. From you is every good thought and desire, every good purpose, every good effort, every good success. It is by you that sinners are turned into saints. It is by you the Church is refreshed and strengthened. Through you new religious orders, new devotions in the Church come into being; new countries are added to the Faith, new manifestations and illustrations are given of the ancient Apostolic creed. I praise and adore you, my Sovereign Lord, the Holy Spirit.

Eighth Day

A Prayer to be a Light to Others

STAY WITH me, and then I shall begin to shine as you shine, so to shine as to be a light to others. The light, O Jesus, will be all from you. It will be you who shines through me upon others. Give light to them as well as to me, light them with me, through me. Make me preach you without preaching - not by words, but by my example and by the sympathetic influence of what I do - by my visible resemblance to your saints, and the evident fullness of the love which my heart bears to you.

Ninth Day

A Prayer for Relatives, Friends & Enemies

JESUS, son of Mary, we pray for all who are near and dear to us. We beg you to bring them all into the light of your truth, or to keep them in your truth if they already know it, and to keep them in a state of grace, and to give them the gift of perseverance. Thus we pray for our fathers and our mothers, for our children, for our brothers and sisters, for our friends, for our neighbours, for our superiors and rulers; for those who wish us well, for those who wish us ill; for our enemies; for our rivals; for our injurers and for our slanderers. And not only for the living, but for the dead, who have died in the grace of God, that He may shorten their time of expiation, and admit them into His presence above.

Tenth Day

A Prayer for an Increase of Faith

MY GOD, you have said that I am more blessed if I believe in you, than if I saw you. Enable me to believe as if I saw; let me have you always before me as if you were always bodily present. Let me ever hold communion with you, my hidden, but my living God.

You are in my innermost heart. Every thought of my mind, every good desire of my heart, is from the presence within me of the unseen God. By nature and by grace you are in me. I see you not in the material world except dimly, but I recognise your voice in my own intimate consciousness. If I am tempted to leave *you*, do not you leave *me*!

Eleventh Day

A Prayer for Unbelievers

O LORD Jesus Christ, upon the Cross you did say: "Father, forgive them, for they know not what they do." And this surely, O my God, is the condition of vast multitudes among us now. They deny that there is a God, but they know not what they are doing. They renounce all faith in you, the Saviour of man. They mislead the wandering, they frighten the weak, they corrupt the young. Others, again, have a wish to be religious, but mistake error for truth - they go after fancies of their own, and they seduce others and keep them from you. They know not what they are doing, but you can make them know. Teach them now, open their eyes here, before the future comes; give them faith in what they must see hereafter, if they will not believe in it here.

Twelfth Day

A Prayer for Christ's Forbearance

O JESU, does any number of falls and relapses vanquish the faithfulness and endurance of your compassion? You forgive not only seven times, but to seventy times seven. And such you are all over the earth, even to the end - forgiving, sparing, forbearing, waiting, though sinners are ever provoking you: pitying and taking into account their ignorance, visiting all men, all your enemies, with the gentle pleadings of your grace, day after day, year after year, up to the hour of their death.

Bear with me in spite of my waywardness, perverseness, and ingratitude. Only give me your grace. Then I shall have happy days in your presence.

Thirteenth Day

A Prayer to Obtain Eternal Life

I BELIEVE and know that all things live in you. Whatever there is of being, of life, of excellence, of enjoyment, of happiness, in the whole of creation, is, in its substance, simply and absolutely yours. It is by dipping into the ocean of your infinite perfections that all beings have whatever they have of good. All that is wonderful in the way of talent or genius is but an unworthy reflection of the faintest gleam of the Eternal Mind. Whatever we do well, is not only by your help, but is an imitation of that sanctity which is in fullness in you. O my God, shall I one day see you? Shall I see the source of that grace which enlightens me, strengthens me, and consoles me? As I came from you, as I am made through you, as I live in you, so may I at last return to you, and be with you for ever and ever.

Fourteenth Day

A Prayer to Bear Suffering Well

MY GREAT GOD, you have humbled yourself and have been lifted up upon the tree! Though I am not fit to ask you for suffering as a gift, at least I will beg of you grace to meet suffering well, when you in your love and wisdom bring it upon me. Let me bear pain, reproach, disappointment, slander, anxiety, suspense, when it comes. I wish to bear insult meekly, and to return good for evil. I wish to humble myself in all things, and to be silent when I am ill used, and to be patient when sorrow or pain is prolonged, and all for the love of you, and your Cross, knowing that in this way I shall gain the promise of this life and of the next.

Fifteenth Day

A Prayer for Wisdom

LORD JESUS, teach me, like Mary, to sit at your feet, and to hear your word. Give me that true wisdom, which seeks your will by prayer and meditation, by direct intercourse with you, more than by reading and reasoning. Give me the discernment to know your voice from the voice of strangers, and to rest upon it and to seek it in the first place, as something external to myself; and answer me through my own mind, if I worship and rely on you as above and beyond it.

Sixteenth Day

A Prayer of Resignation to God's Will

I BELIEVE, my Saviour, that you know just what is best for me. I believe that you love me better than I love myself, that you are all-wise in your Providence, and all-powerful in your protection. My Lord, I will wait on you for your guidance, and, on obtaining it, I will act upon it in simplicity and without fear. And I promise that I will not be impatient, if at any time I am kept by you in darkness and perplexity; nor will I ever complain or fret if I come into any misfortune or anxiety.

Seventeenth Day

A Prayer to Mary, the Mother of Jesus

O HOLY MOTHER, stand by me now at Mass time, when Christ comes to me, as you did minister to your infant Lord. Stand by me, Holy Mother, that I may gain somewhat of your purity, your innocence, your faith, and He may be the one object of my love and my adoration, as He was of yours.

Obtain for me this grace, O Virgin Mother, that I, when I suffer, may associate my sufferings with Him and with you, and that through His passion, and your merits, and those of all Saints, they may be a satisfaction for my sins and procure for me eternal life.

Eighteenth Day

A Prayer for Church Unity

LORD JESUS CHRIST, who, when you were about to suffer, did pray for your disciples to the end of time that they might all be one, as you are in the Father, and the Father in you, break down the walls of separation which divide one party and denomination of Christians from another. Teach all men that the see of St Peter, the Holy Church of Rome, is the foundation, centre, and instrument of unity. Open their hearts to the long-forgotten truth that our Holy Father, the Pope, is your Vicar and Representative; so that as there is but one holy company in heaven above, so likewise there may be one communion, confessing and glorifying your holy name here below.

Nineteenth Day

A Prayer to The Holy Spirit, the Life of The Soul

MY GOD, I adore you, Eternal Paraclete, the light and the life of my soul. You might have been content with merely giving me good suggestions, inspiring grace and helping from without. But in your infinite compassion you have from the first entered into my soul, and taken possession of it. You will go from me, if I sin; and I shall be left to my own miserable self. God forbid; I will use what you have given me; I will call on you when tried and tempted. Through you I will never forsake you.

Twentieth Day

A Prayer for Fervour

IN ASKING for fervour, I ask for all that I can need, and all that you can give. In asking for fervour, I am asking for effectual strength, consistency, and perseverance; I am asking for faith, hope, and charity in their most heavenly exercise. In asking for fervour I am asking to be rid of the fear of man, and the desire of his praise; I am asking for the gift of prayer; I am asking for that loyal perception of duty, which follows on yearning affection; I am asking for sanctity, peace, and joy all at once.

Twenty-First Day

A Prayer for the Faithful Departed

O JESU, Lover of souls, we recommend unto you the souls of all your servants, who have departed with the sign of faith and sleep the sleep of peace. We beseech you, Lord and Saviour, that, as in your mercy to them you became man, so now you would admit them to your presence above.

Gracious Lord, we beseech you, remember not against them the sins of their youth and their ignorances; but be mindful of them in your heavenly glory. May the heavens be opened to them. May the Archangel St Michael conduct them to you. May your holy Angels come forth to meet them, and carry them to the city of the heavenly Jerusalem. May they rest in peace.

Twenty-Second Day

A Prayer to Persevere in the Love of God

WHAT MIND of man can imagine the love which the Eternal Father bears towards the Only Begotten Son? It has been from everlasting - and it is infinite. And now what does He ask of me, but that, as He has loved me with an everlasting love, so I should love Him in such measures as I can show. Complete your work, Lord, and as you have loved me from the beginning, so make me to love you unto the end.

Twenty-Third Day

An Offertory Prayer

MY GOD, I know well, you could have saved us at your word, without yourself suffering; but you did choose to purchase us at the price of your Blood. I look on you, the Victim lifted up on Calvary, and I know that your death was an expiation for the sins of the whole world.

My Lord, I offer you myself in turn as a sacrifice of thanksgiving. You have died for me, and I in turn make myself over to you. My wish is to be separated from everything of this world; to cleanse myself simply from sin. Enable me to carry out what I profess.

Twenty-Fourth Day

A Prayer to the Sacred Heart

MY GOD, my Saviour, I adore your Sacred Heart, for that heart is the seat and source of all your tenderest human affections for us sinners, all your Divine Charity towards us. When you condescend to suffer me to receive you, make my heart beat with your Heart. Purify it of all that is earthly, all that is proud and sensual, all that is hard and cruel. So fill it with you, that in your love and your fear it may have peace.

Twenty-Fifth Day

A Prayer to the Unchangeable God

I KNOW, my God, I must change; if I am to see your face. I must undergo the change of death. Body and soul must die to this world. My real self, my soul, must change by a true regeneration.

Support me, as I proceed in this great, happy change, with the grace of your unchangeableness. Whatever fortune I have, be I rich or poor, healthy or sick, with friends or without, all will turn to evil if I am not sustained by the Unchangeable; all will turn to good if I have Jesus with me, yesterday and today the same, and for ever.

Twenty-Sixth Day

A Holy Communion Prayer

MY GOD, teach me so to live, as one who does believe the great dignity, the great sanctity of that material frame in which you have lodged me. And therefore, O my dear Saviour! do I come so often and so earnestly to be partaker of your Body and Blood, that by means of your own ineffable holiness I may be made holy. Crucify my soul and body in all that is sinful in them, and make me pure as you are pure.

Twenty-Seventh Day

A Prayer to the Holy Spirit, the Fount of Love

MY GOD, I adore you, as the Third Person of the Ever-Blessed Trinity. You are that Living Love, wherewith the Father and the Son love each other. And you are the Author of supernatural love in our hearts. Increase in me this grace of love, in spite of all my unworthiness. It is more precious than anything else in the world. I accept it in place of all the world can give me. It is my life.

Twenty-Eighth Day

A Prayer of Surrender

MY LORD and Saviour, in your arms I am safe; keep me and I have nothing to fear; give me up and I have nothing to hope for. I pray you not to make me rich, I pray you not to make me very poor; but I leave it all to you, because you know and I do not. If you bring pain or sorrow on me, give me grace to bear it well. If you give me health and strength and success in this world, keep me ever on my guard lest these great gifts carry me away from you. Give me ever to aim at setting forth your glory; to live to and for you; to set a good example to all around me; give me to die just at that time and in that way which is most for your glory, and best for my salvation.

Twenty-Ninth Day

A Prayer for Consolation

MY GOD, let me never forget that seasons of consolations are refreshments here, and nothing more. Here they are only intended to prepare us for doing and suffering. I pray you, my God, to give them to me from time to time, lest I go about my daily work in a dry spirit; but let me not rest in them. Let me use them for the purpose for which you give them. Let them carry me forward to the thought and the desire of heaven.

Thirtieth Day

Two Prayers for a Happy Death

MAY HE support us all the day long, till the shades lengthen, and the evening comes, and the busy world is hushed, and the fever of life is over, and our work is done. Then in his mercy may he give us a safe lodging, and a holy rest, and peace at the last.

MY LORD and Saviour, support me in that hour in the strong arms of your Sacraments. Let the absolving words be said over me, and the holy oil sign and seal me, and your own Body be my food. May I receive the gift of perseverance, and die, as I desire to live, in your faith, in your Church, in your service, and in your love. Amen.

Thirty-First Day

A Hymn of Praise

PRAISE to the Holiest in the height,
And in the depth be praise,
In all his words most wonderful,
Most sure in all his ways.

O loving wisdom of our God!
When all was sin and shame,
A second Adam to the fight
And to the rescue came.

O wisest love! that flesh and blood
Which did in Adam fail,
Should strive afresh against their foe,
Should strive and should prevail;

And that a higher gift than grace
Should flesh and blood refine,
God's presence and his very self
And essence all divine.

O generous love! that he who smote
In man for man the foe,
The double agony in man
For man should undergo;

And in the garden secretly,
And on the cross on high,
Should teach his brethren, and inspire
To suffer and to die.

Praise to the holiest in the height,
And in the depth be praise,
In all his words most wonderful,
Most sure in all his ways.

Dream of Gerontius

Lead Kindly Light

LEAD, Kindly Light, amid the encircling gloom
  Lead Thou me on!
  The night is dark, and I am far from home -
    Lead Thou me on!
  Keep Thou my feet; I do not ask to see
  The distant scene - one step enough for me.

I was not ever thus, nor pray'd that Thou
    Shouldst lead me on.
  I loved to choose and see my path, but now
    Lead Thou me on!
  I loved the garish day, and, in spite of fears,
  Pride ruled my will: remember not past years.

So long Thy power hath blest me, sure it still
    Will lead me on,
  Over moor and fen, o'er crag and torrent, till
    The night is gone;
  And with the morn those angel faces smile
  Which I have loved long since, and lost awhile.

Prayer for the Light of Truth

I should like an enquirer to say continually:

MY GOD, I confess that you can enlighten my darkness. I confess that you *alone* can. I *wish* my darkness to be enlightened. I do not know whether you will; but that you can and that I wish, are sufficient reasons for me to *ask*. I hereby promise that by your grace which I am asking, I will embrace whatever I at length feel certain is the truth. And by your grace I will guard against all self-deceit which may lead me to take what nature would have, rather than what reason approves.

Novena

THE Cause for the Canonisation of John Henry Cardinal Newman was opened in 1958 by Archbishop Grimshaw of Birmingham.

It is important for the advancement of the Cause to know of any favours granted through Cardinal Newman's intercession.

Below are readings for nine days, taken from his writings, so that a novena may be made.

First Day

Christin us

THIS is what it is to be one of Christ's little ones . . . to be possessed by his presence as our life, our strength, our merit, our hope, our crown; to become in a wonderful way his members, the instruments, or visible form, or sacramental sign, of the One Invisible Ever Present Son of God, mystically reiterating in each of us all the acts of his earthly life, his birth, consecration, fasting, temptation, conflicts, victories, sufferings, agony, passion, death, resurrection, and ascension; - he being all in all, - we, with as little power in ourselves, as little excellence or merit, as the water in Baptism, or the bread and wine in Holy Communion; yet strong in the Lord and in the power of his might.

Our Father, Hail Mary, Glory be, and the prayer for Canonisation (page 55).

Second Day

The weakness of God

WHEN we confess God as Omnipotent only, we have gained but a half-knowledge of him: his is an Omnipotence which can at the same time swathe itself in infirmity and become the captive of its own creatures. He has, if I may so speak, the incomprehensible power of even making himself weak. We must know him by his Names, Emmanuel and Jesus, to know him perfectly.

Our Father, Hail Mary, Glory be, and the prayer for Canonisation (page 55).

Third Day

God our only Guide

Ibelieve O my Saviour, that you know just what is best for me. I believe that you love me better than I love myself, that you are all-wise in your Providence and all-powerful in your protection. I am as ignorant as Peter was as to what is to happen to me in time to come; but I resign myself entirely to my ignorance, and thank you with all my heart that you have taken me out of my own keeping, and, instead of putting such a serious charge upon me, have bidden me put myself into your hands. I can ask nothing better than this, to be your care, not my own.

Our Father, Hail Mary, Glory be, and the prayer for Canonisation (page 55).

Fourth Day

Waiting on God

WE must not only have faith in him, but must wait on him, not only must hope, but must watch for him; not only love him, but must long for him; not only obey him, but must look out, look up earnestly for our reward, which is himself.

Our Father, Hail Mary, Glory be, and the prayer for Canonisation (page 55).

Fifth Day

Desiring God alone

TO have a virgin soul, is, to love nothing on earth in comparison of God, or except for his sake. That soul is virginal which is ever looking for its Beloved who is in heaven, and which sees him in whatever is lovely upon earth, loving earthly friends very dearly, but in their proper place as his gifts and his representatives... loving Jesus alone with sovereign affection, and bearing to lose all ... [to] keep him.

Our Father, Hail Mary, Glory be, and the prayer for Canonisation (page 55).

Sixth Day

Faith and the world

THE while that we are still on earth, and our duties are in this world, let us never forget that, while our love must be silent, our Faith must be vigorous and lively. Let us never forget that, in proportion as our love is 'rooted and grounded' in the next world, our faith must branch forth like a fruitful tree into this. The calmer our hearts, the more active be our lives; the more tranquil we are, the more busy; the more resigned, the more zealous; the more unruffled, the more fervent.

Our Father, Hail Mary, Glory be, and the prayer for Canonisation (page 55).

Seventh Day

Christic the healer

CHRIST came . . . to gather together in one all the elements of good dispersed throughout the world, to make them his own, to illuminate them with himself, to reform and refashion them into himself. He came to make a new and better beginning of all things than Adam had been, and to be a fountain-head from which all good henceforth might flow.

Our Father, Hail Mary, Glory be, and the prayer for Canonisation (page 55).

Eighth Day

Self-abandonment

IT was a lesson continually set before the Israelites, that they were never to presume to act of themselves, but to wait till God wrought for them, to look on reverently, and then follow his guidance. God was their All-wise King: it was their duty to have no will of their own, distinct from his will, to form no plan of their own, to attempt no work of their own. 'Be still, and know that I am God.' Move not, speak not – look to the pillar of the cloud, see how it moves – then follow. Such was the command.

Our Father, Hail Mary, Glory be, and the prayer for Canonisation (page 55).

Ninth Day

The power of Our Lady's prayer

THIS is why the Blessed virgin is called powerful - nay, sometimes All-powerful, because she has, more than anyone else, more than all Angels and saints, this great, prevailing gift of prayer. No one has access to the Almighty as his Mother has; none has merit such as hers. Her Son will deny her nothing that she asks; and herein lies her power. While she defends the Church, neither height nor depth, neither men nor evil spirits, neither great monarchs, nor craft of man, nor popular violence, can avail to harm us; for human life is short, but Mary reigns above, a Queen forever.

Our Father, Hail Mary, Glory be, and the prayer for Canonisation (page 55).

Prayer for Canonisation of
Cardinal John Henry Newman

God our Father, you granted to your servant
John Henry Newman wonderful gifts of nature
and of grace, that he should be a spiritual light in
the darkness of this world, an eloquent herald of
the Gospel, and a devoted servant of the one
Church of Christ.

With confidence in his heavenly intercession, we
make the following petition: [*here make your petition*].

For his insight into the mysteries of the kingdom,
his zealous defence of the teachings of the Church,
and his priestly love for each of your children, we
pray that he may soon be numbered among the
canonised saints.

We ask this through Christ our Lord.

Please report any favours received to:
The Cause for Newman's Canonisation,
The Oratory, Birmingham B16 8UE, England.

With ecclesiastical approval